# Seasons
## of Four Fathers

Mentor Memoirs of Rondle I. Anderson

A Faith-based Fatherhood Initiative

*Seasons of Four Fathers:*
*Mentor Memoirs of Rondle L. Anderson*

*A Faith-based Fatherhood Initiative*

*Copyright 2014 © by Rondle Anderson, Indiana (USA)*

*ISBN: 978-1523784097*

*For volume orders or speaking engagements, contact:*
*Rondle L. Anderson*
*RLA Consulting Corp*
*P.O. Box 36226*
*Indianapolis, IN 46236*
*E-mail: rlanderson6503@yahoo.com*

*Library of Congress Control Number:  TXU 1 - 916 - 206*

*Book Production, Distribution & Layout*
*Merle Ray, The Noble Groups | Houston, TX*
*www.NobleGroups.com*
*E-mail: mhray@noblegroups.com*
*Phone: 281-827-4396*

# SEASONS OF FOUR FATHERS

*Mentor Memoirs*

*of Rondle L. Anderson*

*A Faith-Based Fatherhood Initiative*

## Mentor Memoirs of Rondle L. Anderson

### Table of Contents

Introduction

Prologue
About the Author
Endorsements

# DEDICATION

This book is first dedicated to the Lord Almighty who gives unmerited favor and wisdom. In my transparency to share life experiences with fathers everywhere, I secondly dedicate this book to my son, Cameron. When I first started writing, he was twenty-six, single, and without children. Cameron was building his career and had decided that marriage and children were a bit down the road. This book was written in part to express to my son the confidence that I had in his abilities as a father when the time came.

Lastly, this book is dedicated to the entire demographic of "daddies" who are incarcerated in correctional facilities. A former warden for over 15 years, I learned that when it comes to child-rearing, these men are living the adage, "absence makes the heart grow fonder." Therefore, this book is dedicated to those men and their offspring as well as mine with the hope that all children may blossom in and from their Seasons of Four Fathers.

# ACKNOWLEDGMENTS

*I would like to thank God for placing me in situations with a purpose to increase my sovereignty toward kingdom building. The following people have also been instrumental throughout this journey:*

- *My mother, Reatha, has dedicated her entire life to help anyone in need. She reared me to always have faith in God and to be strong during times of adversity.*
- *My wife, Nila, has supported and loved me over thirty-four years regardless of the stress she has encountered as she followed my career.*
- *My cousin, Candace, has given her time to read and develop this manuscript while raising two young children.*
- *My son, Cameron, who has supported me with every business related idea and provided me with his own insight.*
- *My daughter, Tanieka, who challenged my spiritual realm through relationships with "seem to be" good men until she finally found the companion sent by God.*
- *My cousin, Apostle Deborah Anderson, inspired me to finish and publish my guide for fatherhood, finished and publishing her own book.*
- *My cousin Andre, who has been a positive role model for all young black males, received his*

*Doctorate in 2012 after several years of adversity.*

- *My Father-in-Law, the late George F. Owens, Sr. who started the Father's Day fishing tradition over twenty-seven years ago.*
- *My church sister, Pam Thomas, who took time out of her busy schedule to critique and help me publish this document;*
- *Last but not least, my Former Commissioner, Edward Cohn, God rests his soul. He believed in my attributes, skills and strengths by appointing me to various Warden Positions.*

# INTRODUCTION

*Fathers come in seasons. I should know; I've been one myself for many years now and have lived long enough to experience all four seasons of fatherhood. There is the rebirth of Springtime when fathers experience new ways to connect with their children and families. Then there is the thrill of mid-year casual days bringing opportunities for some fathers to pop in to a child's life just in time to enjoy the fun-filled hot steamy days of Summer. After that, comes Fall or Autumn when some fathers fall apart when things get tough and leave their children and families for grass that looks greener on the other side. Finally, there's the Winter father who is as sure as the season itself, coming in to bring soundness, stability, traditions, and family values cherished for a lifetime.*

*In this book, I reflect on my own life and the fathers and father-figures that helped to shape who I am today. Whether they were there or not there, the impact of them did not go unnoticed. Just like the seasons, there were four fathers who brought various critical components together in my life. Call me crazy, religious, spiritual, or sentimental, but I'd like to think that God was showing us what fatherhood would be like when He gave us the four seasons. Then, like the Sovereign God that He is, He helps us bring it all together full-circle at* some pre-defined point in our lives. When I thought about it, my life was an example.

I decided to write this book out of concern that fatherhood is becoming a "lost art." I am African-American born in Northwest Indiana and a former Warden of a Maximum Security Prison. I was born in the middle 1950's, right at the cusp of the baby boom generation. There were five other siblings by 1970 in our household: two younger brothers, two younger sisters, and one older sister.

At about the age of five, I remember a light-skinned African-American man stopping by the house. He handed me an orange football. Then after saying a few words to my mother, he disappeared as fast as he had appeared – just like the summertime.

I didn't pay this any mind because a dark-skinned African-American man named Johnny was who all of us knew as "Daddy." Little did I know that he was really my step-father and the father of my four younger siblings. Later, when I did find out the truth, it never mattered to me because my siblings and I only knew each other as brother and sister.

Hopefully, by the end of this book, I will inspire all men who are "Daddies," whether intentional or unintentional, to make child-rearing a priority. Children are of great importance and creating them should not be *a hobby or past-time for seeking thrills. Fatherhood is a "Godsend" and should be cherished as such. Raising children should be as precious and loving as God planned it to be.*

# REDISCOVER THE LOST ART OF FATHERHOOD. LEAVE A POSITIVE IMPRESSION AND IMPACT.

# 1
# IN THE BEGINNING THERE WAS WINTER!

*I know more people born in September than any other month of the year. December cold winters make couples snuggle. I think there's something about the pureness of winter that brings people together. Maybe it's the cold. Maybe it's the beauty of the pure un-driven white snow. But, I think it's no coincidence that God in His Providential Order gave us the Savior Jesus, sometime in the winter before the start of spring as most biblical historians agree. Thus, the vital process of mentoring and family-building for me begins in this season with the deepest of family values.*

*Around the year 1961, I remember Christmas time in northern Indiana. The fluffy white snow that came around Halloween settled in until close to Easter of the following year. Classics like "Winter Wonderland," "Rudolph, the Red Nose Reindeer," and "Frosty the Snowman" were among our favorites to watch on television because they related so well to the outside weather conditions. As children, my siblings and I – not being able to freely roam and gallop outside, were happily confined to the warmth of inside our home.*

*Our house wasn't very large. It had only five rooms: two bedrooms, a living room, bathroom and a kitchen – all of which seemed adequate to me even though two adults and four children lived there. Mom and Daddy Johnny would let the two youngest sleep with them, therefore my older sister and I shared a bedroom which had bunk beds.*

*Siblings five and six had not been born yet. As soon as he was old enough, my younger brother became my bunkbed mate, and my youngest sister got to sleep with Mom and Daddy Johnny all by herself. What a joyful occasion it was for my older sister when Daddy Johnny had the third bedroom built onto the back of the house.*

*Behold, the older sister got the new room! She was just turning fourteen and little did she know this solidarity would be short-lived as the birth of number five, another sister, occurred shortly after the add-on was built. When that occurred in the early 1960's, the shift of bedroom mate siblings started all over again – at least it stayed gender-specific. There were now two girls in the new room, two boys in the second room, and our baby sister with Mom and Daddy. My youngest brother, the sixth sibling was born five years later. Now that I have created this familial portrait, I will get back to winter.*

*I remember like it was yesterday, Daddy Johnny coming home around six o'clock in the evening. He drove a four axle dump truck that he would gear shift twenty-one times to complete a cycle. Our dog, Joe, a mixed border collie would start barking when he heard the sound of the shifting and the diesel engine blaring from a far off distance.*

*The sound of the truck grew louder and louder the closer Daddy Johnny came. Our neighbors were just as excited as we were and would yell out, "Here comes Johnny!" I would smile, and then start pacing and shouting, "Daddy's coming; Daddy's coming!" Daddy Johnny would then roll down the alley behind the house and then turn into the yard. He'd get out of the truck covered in white rock soot from head to toe, and smile as he looked at me. "Hey boy!" He would say and then gently pat me on the head. He proceeded to the house while waving to the next door neighbors who greeted him with a "Hi, Johnny!"*

*Another memory was when Daddy Johnny came home from hunting. He would go somewhere in Michigan between Thanksgiving and Christmas. He always had a nice deer strapped to the front hood of his car when he returned. I listened to him brag to our neighbor and friend next door saying, "Thirty off six did it again!" He loved talking about his favorite rifle! Daddy Johnny would then take the deer away for processing and return routinely with a live Christmas tree. I would get the tree stand from the utility room with much excitement.*

*This was a seasonal tradition that made me very happy. Daddy Johnny would show his appreciation by saying, "Thanks, boy!" Then directing his attention to Mom, he'd say, "It's all yours to decorate." Mom would then pop the popcorn in a big stew pot and get out the box of Christmas ornaments.*

*She provided black thread to string the popcorn and watched us closely so as not to eat the freshly made decoration. These winter time moments were custom and annual. We looked forward to them as much as getting a pillowcase full of candy at Halloween and new clothes for Easter. These family memories became traditions that Daddy Johnny instilled during the season. They were very pleasant times that made our family forget about poverty and strife. As the seasons moved on, some traditions were maintained while others slipped away.*

*Wintertime, however, provided a great opportunity for me and my siblings to be mentored as children. There was closeness due to the outside elements that kept us inside the majority of the time. There were multiple opportunities to play table or board games such as checkers, dominos, chess, Monopoly, Scrabble and even something as simple as "Go Fish!" I remember playing a game with my siblings and Daddy Johnny called "Sorry." It was a simple game of moving from one space to another according to the numbers on the dice.*

*Another winter values opportunity was the sharing of the birth of Christ in December. Instead of the hustle and bustle of shopping and being driven by material things, we were taught that this Miracle was the true meaning of Christmas. My siblings and I would be encouraged by Mom and Daddy Johnny to watch television shows such as the "Ten Commandments," "Charlie Brown's Christmas," "Miracle on 34th Street," and a "Christmas Carol." We sang songs such as "It Came upon a Midnight Clear," "Joy to the World," and "Silent Night." I have carried on this tradition with my children and grandchildren because I treasure the culture and values it developed during my childhood. Over the years however, watching the delight of my grandchildren, I may have traded the "Christmas Carol" for the "Polar Express." But, the joyful times and season of remembrance from my winters with my family and the Christian values we shared will always be the starting point for the memories we share and teach our own kids. Values like sharing, caring, and giving to others in need were the foundational principles that Mom, Daddy Johnny, and our strong extended family of supporters taught us, and these values remain with us even today.*

# CREATE STABLE MEMORIES AND TRADITIONS WORTH HOLDING ON TO.

# WINTERTIME PROVIDES A GREAT OPPORTUNITY FOR CHILDREN TO BE MENTORED.

# 2
# AH SPRING!

*The spring season, starting with Easter and our "new duds" left memories that were spiritual. Even though Mom encouraged church participation all throughout the year, Sunday worship was especially mandatory. Therefore, we'd spend much of Saturday evening just preparing for the following Sunday morning.*

*I remember the smell of hot grease and burnt hair coming from our kitchen on Saturday evenings. My sisters, starting with the oldest, would sit in a chair while Mom heated up the "straightening comb" on the stove. I also observed this same ritual at my Aunt Lenora's house when my brother and I would sleep over.*

*Daddy Johnny also got into a particular practice on Saturday evenings. He would place my younger brother, who we called "Junior" and I on a folding chair that was kept on the back porch. He plugged in his hair clippers to the overhead light and then went to work on us one head at a time. I don't think Mom or Dad went to Beauty or Barber's School, because of the scent of our sisters' burnt hair and the "bowl haircuts" that both Junior and I received. We looked like sheep after the shearers, but we didn't know any better! We had grown accustomed to this tradition because it was part of the work and preparation that our parents did a whole day in* advance just to prepare all of us for Sunday worship services the next day.

Daddy Johnny didn't go to church with us. My Uncle Charlie, who was a Deacon, would pick us up because Mom didn't drive. Uncle Charlie and his wife, Aunt Bee, kept us kids close to them to ensure complete compliance of our behavior while sitting on the church pew. We were quiet as mice!

I remember being afraid of Uncle Charlie at first when he and Aunt Bee started watching over us in their home while my mother worked. Uncle Charlie assumed the role of daddy while we were in their care. Sometimes I wondered where Daddy Johnny was that made us have to be at Uncle Charlie's and Aunt Bee's so much. Nevertheless, I obeyed Uncle Charlie even though I didn't understand why he had to be in charge.

We knew nothing of the philosophy of a "village raising a child" but that is what was really going on. Even though I was not sure where Daddy Johnny was or what he was doing, I became very secure with Uncle Charlie and Aunt Bee. They instilled a family atmosphere and took every opportunity to talk to us about loving each other and encouraging us to enjoy just being kids.

Their house was a quaint single story bungalow that was located in a low crime area. There was a piano in the house, but I don't recall either of them playing it.

However, Christian music was played on the radio every time we visited because they loved church. I would frequently hear hymns being sung and prayers to God about everything they were blessed with, including my two sisters and brother.

During the winter, Uncle Charlie and Aunt Bee had just given birth to a lovely baby girl. Their house also had a couple of bedrooms, but they had a room that Aunt Bee used as a den to sew clothes and get away from the five of us to enjoy her serenity.

As a child I had chronic asthma, thus one of my fondest spring memories is that of my Aunt and Uncle embracing me when my asthma flared up. Aunt Bee and Uncle Charlie would pray as they rocked me back and forth. All the attention was on helping me breathe as I pumped the inhaler.

They both caressed me and rocked me back and forth until I seemed okay. Aunt Bee had asthma as well; therefore she seemed to be the medical expert when I had problems. Her remedy, when she experienced difficulty breathing, was to escape to her den. In there would be a large pot giving off smoke fumes that she inhaled. Uncle Charlie would direct us outside while she medicated herself.

Thinking back on this season, it's ironic how springtime led to fresh air, however, Aunt Bee and I *struggled to breathe due to our asthma. During the spring we spent a lot of time with our Aunt and Uncle. We didn't realize anything significant was going on between Mom and Daddy Johnny.*

*Back at home, Mom loved to cook. Her first job that I could remember was cleaning floors in a "Big Boy" restaurant. Soon she started doing short order cooking after the floors were done. She boasted about her boss and how appreciative she was for him giving her the opportunity. She referred Aunt Bee to her boss, but Aunt Bee only worked one day before she decided that babysitting and raising kids was more rewarding.*

*Spring would end with memories of Daddy Johnny bringing home animals as he returned from his periodic disappearances. I remember once he brought home a live snapping turtle, a pheasant and a raccoon. The 'coon,' as he called it, was dead and so were the pheasants. He would tie the snapping turtle to the front bumper of his dump truck and delighted us as he stuck large twigs in its mouth so that the turtle could snap them in half. It was entertaining, but as I think back to that time, he was really showing me and my siblings how dangerous the animal could be if we got too close.*

*He would then summon for our next door neighbor, who enjoyed cutting up the turtle for turtle soup. We never saw Daddy Johnny clean the pheasants or the coons but we speculated that our neighbors did that part also. Sometimes when Daddy Johnny entered the house he would give Mom money and say, "Here you go Rita; get the kids some groceries." Mom would smile and put the money away. She would be cooking supper and my older sister would assist her while my brother and I stayed outside riding our bikes until we were called in the house to eat, which was usually around six o' clock in the evening.*

*Another warm-hearted memory of spring was the rain showers we received in northern Indiana. I remember Mom dressing me up in a yellow raincoat, yellow hat, and a pair of goulashes. Not realizing at the time, I looked like the kid on the Morton salt box! Mom would send my older sister and me to elementary school. Daddy Johnny would complain by saying, "Rita you got that boy looking stupid!" Mom, however, because of my asthma would reply, "Oh Johnny, Go somewhere. I don't want him getting sick!"*

*My oldest sister and I walked to and from school like all of the other kids in the neighborhood. There were no yellow buses unless you had to ride the little yellow bus, which we called "the short bus." Sometimes Daddy Johnny would joke with Junior and I when we did something careless and comment, "If you keep on doing that, you will be riding the short bus!" We would quickly stop because kids in the neighborhood always made fun of the students on the bus.*

*Springtime left memories that were synonymous with "new beginnings." Winter was cold and desolate, while springtime sprouted new leaves, green grass and the first bloom of flowers after the much needed spring rain showers. Mentoring is a way to improve and help mentored children learn new things and enhance their current learning abilities. Current Dads and "Dads to be" should be mentoring and renewing relationships with their children just like springtime renews all things that became stagnant in the winter.*

*There are multiple opportunities to engage a child such as spring sports and numerous outdoor activities. The parks and recreation departments open their doors to families on spring break from school. Recreation establishments, such as roller skating rinks, fishing lakes, baseball fields and go-karts provide optimal space and time. I have thoroughly enjoyed fishing with my son in the past and now currently with my grandsons. However, I don't get to catch many fish because of constantly baiting their hooks, untangling fishing lines, and helping them get the caught fish off the hook. This leaves little time to put my line in the water, but being with them is priceless.*

*Mentoring is a lot like fishing. I may not get to cover all the things that I want to do because of constantly being there for the kids, helping them untangle their 'fishing lines of life' and helping them get on and stay on the right track in life. As I am older now this leaves little time for me to cover all the things that I sometimes plan to do, but being there for the kids is priceless!*

*Learning arts and craft skills in the park such as pottery and making necklaces out of beads used to be popular in my time but seems to be lost in today's times. I don't want to lose this culture so I take my grandsons to the local YMCA. At the "Y" children can engage in some of the old cultures that I am familiar with. We still go swimming, shoot some "hoops" and partake in the arts and crafts that are offered at the "Y."*

*In the past, I tried to instill work ethics and responsibility with my son by teaching him to cut grass, trim shrubs/bushes, rake leaves, paint the deck and wash cars. Some of these chores were mandatory and repetitious before he could "hang out" with his peers. I recall a time when he decided to test these responsibilities, but he soon found out that I did not believe in "sparing the rod." Needless to say, disobedient behavior was not repeated in the future.*

*Cameron and I would also keep very busy with extra-curricular activities such as "Pop Warner" football, Little League basketball and baseball, middle school track and field, middle school basketball and high school football and basketball. He also enjoyed music so I kept him involved in school band from middle school to high school. I loved to see the dedication and motivation he displayed while participating in all of these activities. He didn't quit and experienced success which I believe is currently paying off. I hope that repeating these types of responsibilities with my grandsons will also be beneficial.*

# MENTORING IS LIKE FISHING. BE THERE TO UNTANGLE THEIR LINES.

# 3
# SUMMERTIME FUN!

*A Faith-Based Fatherhood Initiative*

*Memories of summertime included staying over Uncle Preacher and Aunt Lenora's house. They seemed to have enough bedrooms to accommodate my older sister, my brother and I. At that time, their three boys and four girls as well as the three of us seemed to have plenty of room. My older sister along with Junior and I would practically live there so we didn't have to share space at home. The irony is that we shared our cousin's rooms and were just as cramped. We didn't care, however, because we always had fun.*

*The house was a two story "Leave it to Beaver" house only a couple of miles from our home. It appeared that it was Uncle Preacher and Aunt Lenora's turn to be part of the village, especially during summer months. We were out of school so Junior and I would wake up early, get dressed and then ride our bikes to their house. Our friends were few as we grew up, because we had each other and our male cousins over Uncle Preacher's house.*

*We could get away by going to Pulaski Park which was just across the street. The park had workers who taught us pottery, crochet and using beads to make necklaces. We thought it also had a small cement swimming pool but it actually was just a big cement fountain. We would jump in it from time to time to stay cool. We also played basketball until dark. However, being the kids that we were, all of our ideas were not safely thought through.*

*We ended up witnessing a tragedy. One of our friends fell off a moving train while we were all trying to "hop it." Our friend lost both of his legs from the knee down. We ran to the nearest house for someone to call 911. When the ambulance arrived, our friend survived, but ended up being a paraplegic the rest of his life. We tended to be somewhat rebellious during this time. We knew right from wrong, but ignored certain rules if the task at hand seemed to be more fun or exciting than the rule. For example, ignoring curfew was a common violation. Hindsight now tells me that the tragedy would have been avoided if we were home being supervised rather than hopping trains past dawn. Being boys we made decisions on what popped into our minds. The days were longer and hotter in the summer which gave us an excuse to be mischievous without parental supervision.*

*For the time being, Daddy Johnny would come by to check on us but never insisted that we come home. He wouldn't stay long because it appeared that he didn't get along well with Uncle Preacher, who was Mom's brother. Uncle Preacher spent most of his time cultivating a huge garden. He raised just about every vegetable you could imagine and spent hours picking weeds so that the garden looked presentable. The surrounding neighbors would all get their vegetables from Uncle Preacher, although he saved most of the vegetables for his own family and siblings. My uncle also worked hard to raise his family. He worked for an asphalt company and would come home after hot summer days with tar all over his boots and his clothes smelled the same way. This was pretty much every day during the week while still keeping his garden in good condition. However, on weekends we didn't see much of him, especially at night.*

ENSURE THAT YOUR CHILD FEELS LOVED AND PROTECTED.

*Mom would make sure we didn't wear out our welcome with our aunt and uncle. She would summon us home, even though Junior and I would ride our Stingray bikes back over there each day. Uncle Charlie and Aunt Bee would also make sure we returned home so that we wouldn't miss Sunday school.*

*Daddy Johnny found chores for us around the house when we did stay home. He had Junior and I cut the grass, trim bushes, paint and wash his vehicles. He loved sparkling clean vehicles, especially his big red dump truck. Besides his truck, he had two cars and a Jeep.*

*All of his vehicles were only a couple of years old. He loved Chryslers and Cadillacs. The Chrysler Imperial actually had an oval steering wheel and push buttons on the dash. He used his Jeep to get around in the winter and to take us fishing at Lake Michigan. I inherited the 1964 Cadillac Deville when I started high school.*

*We didn't realize that a village of relatives was raising us all year long, particularly in the summers. We felt loved and protected and the adult men in our lives were the disciplinarians. Punishments were harsh and sometimes scars were left, but none of us, including our cousins, wanted for anything.*

*Summertime was fun, but as I approached my middle teens, I began to become rebellious. Daddy Johnny's presence was less visual, so Mom had to perform both roles while at home. She forbade me and my sister from going to house parties, but we would sneak out and go anyway. We knew Mom was tired from working and raising kids so we would convince her that we were visiting friends.*

*My older sister would end up going out with her boyfriend and I'd hang out with the neighborhood boys. We showed up at parties, got into fights, and at times vandalized a person's property without remorse. There were however, many consequences to this behavior.*

*One time I ended up in the juvenile court for violation of curfew and property damage. Another was being arrested for possession of stolen property. When that happened, Mom would then call Uncle Charlie who would bring her to the Juvenile Center to bring me home. I didn't get a spanking but Uncle Charlie prayed the whole ride home. The prayer must have worked because my court hearing ruled for me to leave Northern Indiana and enroll in college upon graduation of high school.*

*There are a lot of opportunities in the summer to mentor your sons and daughters. As mentioned earlier, fishing, playing sports, bike riding and simply picnicking in the back yard promotes positive growth. Without these types of interactions, kids like me would engage in negative behavior, hangout with the wrong crowd and even end up a prodigy of the Criminal Justice System. Being absent from your child physically or spiritually during those adolescent years could be very harmful.*

# ABSENT SUMMERTIME MENTORING KIDS TEND TO ENGAGE IN RISKY ACTIVITIES OR NEGATIVE BEHAVIOR.

# THERE ARE LOTS OF OPPORTUNITIES TO MENTOR A CHILD AT ANY AGE.

# 4
# FALL APART!

*A Faith-Based Fatherhood Initiative*

*As I think back, I can relate the fall season to "falling apart." Not so much in our early years, but later on as we grew up as teenagers. Daddy Johnny was less visible, Mom was working harder and their relationship began to change. There were signs of resentment. We could hear Mom and Daddy Johnny arguing at night, even to the point of physically fighting. We didn't know what they were arguing about at the time, but many curse words were used and Daddy Johnny would storm out of the house in the middle of the night.*

*The five of us would climb into bed with Mom. Often times she would be crying. "Everything will be okay," she would assure us. "Your daddy is going through some hard times." One night we noticed a butcher's knife under her pillow. Everything changed after that night. We hardly saw Daddy Johnny anymore until he came back to help us move out of the house. We had been raised in that house and it was awfully strange seeing my mother have to put a knife under her pillow for protection.*

*Daddy Johnny had developed health problems that kept him from driving his truck. As a result, he had lost his job. He and Mom ended up having to declare bankruptcy, which in turn caused the loss of our house. Daddy Johnny had also been "sleeping around" and was caught by Mom with one of her waitresses. The waitress told Mom that she was pregnant with Daddy Johnny's child. After that, we moved to another house on the south side of town.*

*We all had to change schools and make new friends, except for my baby sister. The new house was larger than our old one, but there weren't many kids in the neighborhood to play with. Junior and I spent more time over Uncle Preacher's house, which in our minds wasn't 'broken' like ours.*

*Unfortunately over time we learned that Uncle Preacher and Aunt Lenora were having the same arguments and fights our parents were having. Aunt Lenora would cry after fighting with our uncle. They would argue about the amount of time he spent away from home, and soon Junior and I found ourselves hearing familiar ringtones from the same experiences Mom and Daddy Johnny had at our home.*

*Mom and Daddy Johnny continued to have marital problems even at the new house. They became more distant with each other, talking less and occupying the house when the other was absent. The arguments as we knew them slowed down, but it was obvious they were growing apart.*

*My older sister would also start having conflicts with Daddy Johnny. She was approaching the age of eighteen and wanted to "hang out" with her friends.*

*Daddy Johnny did not agree with this, and I remember a serious argument when she came home later than he expected. The argument became so physical that at one point, she threw a table lamp at Daddy Johnny. She then shouted "You are not my Daddy and can't tell me what to do!" My sister then vowed she was leaving as soon as she turned eighteen. Shortly after that altercation we moved again, this time, without Daddy Johnny.*

*We moved into Uncle Charlie and Aunt Bee's house, even though they didn't have enough room for all of us. Daddy Johnny would come by on occasion to visit and try to "mend fences." Mother was a 'hard sell' for a long time. The three of us (my older sister, Junior, and I) would spend more time with Uncle Preacher and Aunt Lenora due to the lack of space at Uncle Charlie and Aunt Bee's.*

*As time went on, Mom was blessed with a home of her own a couple of blocks away from Aunt Bee and Uncle Charlie. It was a modest two story five room house, which included three bedrooms and an attic. Mom's bedroom was on the main floor and the other two bedrooms were upstairs next to the attic.*

*My oldest sister got the large bedroom upstairs, while my two youngest received the middle sized room. Junior and I decided to move into the attic. Shortly thereafter, Daddy Johnny and Mom made up and she let him move back in. He had a smaller dump truck and found work with a local company. Daddy Johnny came home every day, provided groceries and helped to pay utility bills. There was one difference however, and that was a noticeable drinking of alcohol.*

*We were once again a fully united family until my oldest sister's eighteenth birthday. As promised she married the day after her birthday and moved into her own apartment with her husband, just as she had vowed eight months earlier.*

*Fall was an extremely active and chaotic time. A part of us left when my sister left. I became the oldest child with all of the responsibilities. Dishes had to be washed, floors swept and trash taken out. I would always take Junior with me to take out the trash. He would hold the shovel so that when I kicked the barrel, he could hit the rat that routinely jumped out. I would hurry to dump the trash in the barrel and then Junior and I would run back in the house.*

*Daddy Johnny and Mom knew about the rodents but insisted all chores being done before they came home from work. If not, I would be subject to a whipping from Mom first and then Daddy Johnny who came home a couple of hours later. I did "call their bluff" once but, painfully found out it wasn't worth it.*

*Another chore in the fall was for Junior and I to each get a five gallon can and then walk about a mile to the Fuel Oil Store to get fuel oil for our fifty-gallon oil container behind the house. This was the only way to heat our house for the colder months during the upcoming winter. The trip to the Fuel Oil Store became a daily function for us, since we could only carry ten gallons at a time. Daddy Johnny would praise me, but scold Junior for spilling fuel oil from his five-gallon can, even though Junior was only ten years old at the time. I also remember Daddy telling Junior on more than one occasion that he was no good and needed to be more like his big brother. I didn't realize it at the time, but the resentment toward Junior could have been directly related to the fact that I was not Daddy Johnny's biological son. It appeared he desired a competitive edge for Junior and wanted him to be better because Junior was his biological son. I believe that this ridicule contributed to some negativity that Junior experienced later in life.*

*Chores were an everyday responsibility for all of us. We didn't get any money for carrying out these tasks, unlike kids today who think a monetary reward is necessary. We learned the value of being responsible. Instilling a good work ethic was the one constant principle that Daddy Johnny and my Uncles all possessed.*

# 5
# PURPOSEFUL DIRECTIONS

*A Faith-Based Fatherhood Initiative*

*Men who "live life on the edge" or become incarcerated after having children should also take heed of the seasons of fatherhood. It is a rude awakening that I have seen of adult men all too often who get to prison only to find out that the illegal activities they were involved in, sadly took precedent over their children. Thousands of innocent children, boys and girls left living in a mental prison of their own. Sadly they go to bed every night and wake up every morning asking the question, "Where's my Daddy?"*

*The story I will leave you with, is one such story of a juvenile that I met early on in my corrections career. He was incorrigible at home and ran away several times. The interesting thing about him was his ability to communicate and willingness to follow rules while incarcerated. Several staff would ask me to let him do errands because he did not "push back." Eventually he was release from the juvenile facility to a foster placement. I then met him again, after receiving a promotion to another location. However, this facility was an Adult Medium Security prison. He told me that he ran away again and burglarized a residence to obtain money to survive. He was now sentenced to four years behind bars.*

*While incarcerated he again became the "managers pet" because of his willingness to help. He rarely got into trouble, so the "halo affect" was present with the staff. I can remember him helping an investigation involving staffs who were trafficking (bringing unauthorized items) with other inmates. He served his time and was again released. The third encounter with this young man came as I walked the ranges of "Death Row" as the Warden of the State Prison. There he was in the cell sitting on his bunk with his head in his hands. He looked up at me and stated, "I sure have messed up now!" I responded back, "Yes, you have!"*

*When I got back to my office I read his file to enlighten myself on his crime. The information was startling. He decided to commit robberies on patrons of highway rest stops.*

*Unfortunately one of his victims was a Pastor who would not give in to his wishes. He ended up fatally shooting the Pastor and his wife. Once he was apprehended and convicted, the Judge, looking at his history, saw no other recourse than to sentence him to death by lethal injection.*

*When the time came for his execution we again dialogued about the past. He talked about the times he was a prison clerk and did what he had to do to get out. I admitted to him that I didn't try hard enough to turn him around because of the "halo effect." We shed a tear, shook hands and went through the process. He was the last execution that I facilitated and probably the most memorable.*

*As I look back on that experience, I can't help but to believe that God's purpose throughout my existence on earth was to make a difference in a child's life through mentoring. I can't help but to imagine what this young man's life might have been like had his father been an active presence in his life. God's assignment, I believe, for me throughout my career in the department, was to see innocent and abandoned children without a father-figure in their lives, and to do my best to make a difference. I watch over my grandsons very closely so that they do not become "victims of the streets" or subjected to violence.*

*The experience of this young man showed me the ultimate impact of complacent men who are not serious about child-rearing or mentoring. The game we used to play with Daddy Johnny called Sorry emphasized how a player's direction could be changed by one throw of the dice. If someone threw the dice and landed where you were, all they would say is 'Sorry' and you would be sent all the way back to the starting point. If the dice kept landing on your position, you would eventually lose the game. That's a sad picture of this young man's life. The absence of a father in his life was equivalent to rolling the dice. Three times the young man was sent back into the criminal justice system because the father that he never knew rolled the dice with his son's life by walking away, in effect by all observable means, saying 'Sorry.'*

'FALLS' ARE SOMETIMES INEVITABLE IN LIFE; BUT HAVING FATHER-FIGURES IN ONE'S LIFE HELPS TO SOFTEN THE BLOW.

# DON'T ROLL THE DICE WITH YOUR CHILD'S LIFE. BE PURPOSEFUL.

# 6
# REFLECTIONS OF SEASONS

*Ecclesiastes 3:1 says "To everything there is a Season, a time for every purpose under Heaven." Ecclesiastes, in my opinion, describes how my family faced different seasons of joy, love, pain, growth and fellowship. We didn't know that we were under privileged, because we never felt under privileged. We thought everyone had subsidized food and shopped at the local 'Goodwill.' Our life's purpose was spent primarily taking care of each other's needs based on our love for one another. This was especially true during joyful seasons like Christmas and Summer. However, there is no growth without pain or struggle. This we experienced in other seasons, especially Fall.*

*All four of the fathers mentioned in my story (Daddy Johnny, Uncle Preacher, the light-skinned African American and Uncle Charlie) had plans of being great fathers. As I got to know them over the years, I found that in the early years of their relationships and marriages, it seemed their intentions were good. However, as time went by, the persistence, perseverance, endurance and sheer grit that it takes to be a Dad would prove that each season comes with challenge.*

*For example, Daddy Johnny instilled the value of providing for your family regardless of circumstances. He greeted me with a smile every day and a show of affection even though he had been working in the construction field which was very hard manual labor. This made me feel cherished and important. But Daddy Johnny ended up having affairs with other women when he was absent from our family. His affairs resulted in impregnating two women other than Mom. This left our family feeling betrayed as my siblings and I struggled to understand abandonment*

*Uncle Preacher was gambling when he disappeared on weekends. When questioned by my Aunt, he became physically abusive. He thought that simply bringing home extra money was enough to maintain a great relationship. His obsession led to a separation from his family that was never reconciled.*

*Uncle Charlie was the only father who kept his family together all four seasons. His love for Christ, Aunt Bee and his family (in that order) was steadfast. He and Aunt Bee taught us that prayer is a value that keeps us rooted and grounded across our years. Through their teaching about prayer, I learned that 'Our Father, who art in heaven' provided us mercy and grace throughout our lives. Because of Uncle Charlie's steadfastness in role-modeling prayer before me, I came to know the power of prayer as a valuable tool to overcome adversity. Learning to pray also gave me the peace of mind and faith that my children would be successful in life.*

*Not only a steadfast man, Uncle Charlie was also a disciplinarian, but he always displayed his love to our family in many ways. One way was by taking us in to live with them when Mom and Dad separated. Uncle Charlie believed in Genesis 1:28 which talks about our purpose to be fruitful and multiply. He believed in the scriptures that teach us that our seed should not be sewn recklessly.*

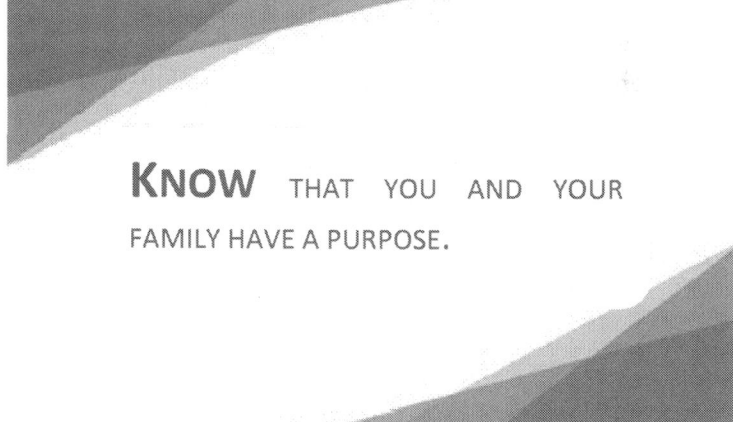

KNOW THAT YOU AND YOUR FAMILY HAVE A PURPOSE.

*Now recall the "light skinned man" mentioned at the beginning of my story. It turned out that he was my biological father. There were rumors and hints from high school classmates that I had brothers and sisters going to the same school, but I ignored them. The rumors to me were just that, rumors! However, in the late 1990's, my biological father introduced himself. He sent me articles of his siblings and information on upcoming family reunions.*

*What he didn't know was that my oldest sister told me all about him approximately ten years earlier. I didn't reach out to him back then because my mom, Daddy Johnny and my siblings were the only real family that I knew. The thought of being around relatives, especially a new Dad that I did not know made me uncomfortable. And besides, being raised around Uncle Charlie, I believed that simply having babies by many different women was reckless, so it took me some time to respond to this invitation of a new family. Later on, I was happy that I did.*

*From this experience, I learned that we should instill the seriousness of family responsibility to our children. What I mean by that is we as men and parents should show them how to prioritize what's first in life when they think of conceiving a child. We should become role models ourselves that invest in our families showing that families do matter. When we do this we demonstrate the value of having a positive role model and father figure.*

## SHOW YOUR CHILD HOW TO PRIORITIZE WHAT'S FIRST IN LIFE. BE A ROLE MODEL.

*I also learned that our parents will sometimes forsake us. My biological father was absent in my life and the man who I called Daddy was a provider, but he became interested in fathering other children away from his own home. By those two examples, I could have gone down the wrong path. But God showed me how to be a father by becoming a father to me.*

*My son and daughter have grown up and started their own families. I have been blessed with three beautiful grandsons and a granddaughter. I enjoy taking them to the same positive activities that I had a privilege to experience. Outside, especially in Northern Indiana, I recall sledding down snowy hillsides with my grandson during my latter years. He and I both screamed as we enjoyed the thrill of the 'unknown' at the bottom of the hill. I will also enjoy mentoring my Son's first child when she is old enough to remember.*

# 7
# SPIRITUAL FATHERING

*If it wasn't for the upbringing and love from my Mother and Uncle, there probably would not have been teachings about God, who I came to know as Father of all fathers. I have learned that my true Father throughout my years was actually the Lord Almighty. He sent different men to mentor me at different times and never forsook me Himself. The spiritual guidance I received has been passed on to my son and daughter so that they know their Daddy and their true Father who is God Almighty!*

*I am grateful to God for allowing me to live to see my son, Cameron, take fatherhood seriously. I also have further hopes and prayers that the inmates God has allowed me to institutionally steward throughout the years have begun to do the same. It is my hope that their relationships with their significant others mature to the understanding that bringing a child into the world is a livable conceivable reality, privilege, and crucial responsibility.*

*The beginning of fatherhood is more than just "three minutes of feel-good." The short act of pleasure produces a begotten being that needs love, companionship, and leadership from a mother and a father. When one of these variables is missing, the child only gets half the love and training he needs from home. The other half usually results in bonding with peers, memberships, and influences, both positive and negative. Unfortunately, for many of the men who are locked up (and their children), these associated influences were gangs, illegal drugs, and worse.*

*It is apparent to me now that God placed me in a purposeful position within the Department of Corrections. As stated earlier, He provided me a way to attend college even though my parents were low income after my Dad became ill. He placed me in a juvenile home as a houseparent for wayward boys after college. God then set me to work in the Department of Correction as a Correctional Officer, even though I had already obtained a college degree. He then provided career opportunities within the department, ranging from Counselor up to Warden, eventually ending with the overall responsibility of supervising Wardens across the state as the departments Regional Director.*

## MENTORING YOUR SON OR DAUGHTER IS A MUST!

*Today I am still involved with mentoring. Our Church Pastor appointed me as the leader of the Mentoring Faculty. We have established relationships with the public school system of Indianapolis which has blessed our church with a school adoption program. I have also maintained leadership roles with the Criminal Justice Association in mentoring future board members.*

*As I stated at the beginning of this book, God has a way of leading you full-circle through the seasons of fatherhood. I believe my full-circle came when I was able to be there for my biological father in his last hours of life even though he was not able to be there for me as his son.*

*As I sat next to my biological father while he was in hospice, I felt a closeness that I hadn't felt before. He couldn't respond, but I know he heard me finally say, "I love you Dad," and that it was okay for him to "Go on to a peaceful glory." At that moment tears rolled down my face and my heart became heavy instead of cold. I felt my heart break from twenty years of memories starting from the day he introduced himself at the reunion. It was the same feeling I had when attending the funeral of Daddy Johnny.*

*I believe that children today feel the same way when their fathers are absent due to incarceration, finding another family, or simply being a "dead-beat" Dad. Mentoring your son or daughter routinely and consistently in my opinion is a must, whether you are present in the home or away due to circumstances. I still needed a wholesome upbringing with the understanding that my real dad loved me and would protect me when I needed support.*

*Getting to know and understand my biological father gave me a chance to love him like a son should love his father. In Philippians 1, Paul states, "Your love will abound more and more in knowledge and in all discernment." To me, this says that the more I know about a person, the more opportunities I have to grow in love and understanding toward them. This is how it felt to be at my father's bedside for him in his last hours. I was there as a son without anger or hard-feelings for all the previous years. I knew then that I had been richly blessed to meet him and to have that opportunity to love him.*

*Most assuredly, I have come to the conclusion that no matter who one's biological father or father figure is, God is Father of all. He is the Good Father — available at all times whenever you need Him and indeed there whenever you think you don't. He is the gift-giver: providing strength, courage, and grace that carries us in good times and bad. You can go boldly to him in confidence because of the relationship and identity you have with Him.*

## OUR FATHER GOD SET THE

### GOLD STANDARD FOR MENTORING.

*I am reminded of the example that young Jesus displayed when He went to the temple in Jerusalem. He*

*had chosen to stay there when the rest of the camp had left. Out of excitement Jesus had failed to let his earthly father and mother, Joseph and Mary, know that he was lagging behind. When his parents realized that he was missing, they rushed back to Jerusalem frightful that they had lost him forever. But the lad Jesus was found doing His Father's business teaching and sharing the Father's love in the temple.*

*When questioned why he had worried his parents and indeed the whole group that was with them, by not keeping up with the rest of the camp, Jesus told Joseph that He was born to be in His Father's house doing His Father's business. Jesus savored His relationship with the Father God so much that He regarded His Heavenly Father's business as His own business. This was because of the relationship that Jesus experienced with the Heavenly Father even as a young lad. Jesus had come to realize even at this early age, that He could trust and depend on the Heavenly Father for everything. That is why He was not afraid when the rest of the caravan had left the temple and He chose to stay behind. Though he submitted Himself to his earthly parents when they located him and joyfully went back home with them, Jesus had become empowered by the close communion that He enjoyed with the Lord. – This is the same sweet fellowship that would follow Him all the way through to His adulthood.*

Our Father God set the gold standard of what it means to lead and mentor a son or daughter. He covered Jesus from divine conception to birth. Natural and biological fathers should cover their seed in the same manner. We should not condone and allow our seed to be wasted seed; our very seed was designed to be fertile for a reason – to serve a godly purpose on earth. From birth through childhood and from childhood to adulthood, we should be there for our children. They should know who we are – even down to our very temperaments. They should be so enamored by the way we love them that they want to mimic our very nature. Ultimately, we should teach them how to triumph over death and the grave unto eternal life just like the Heavenly Father directed Jesus' path to and through the cross.

Earthly fathers should lead and mentor their children so that the children can display and demonstrate the same gold standard of leadership. If we as fathers demonstrate God's way of covering our children, taking care of our children, and being there to guide and direct, cherish and nurture our children, then our children will feel accountable to walk in our footsteps, just as men and women on earth should feel accountable to walk in God's footsteps. When we as fathers do this, then our children in turn will savor their relationships with us as fathers.

*List of Cited References:*

*Holy Bible (NKJV)*

*Johnny L. Powell, Sr (Stepfather-Deceased)*
*Dennis Anderson (Uncle - Deceased)*
*Charlie Bland   (Uncle - Deceased)*
*Ronnie B. Bland (Aunt - Deceased)*
*Nila J. Anderson (Wife)*
*Elmer Joseph, Sr (Biological Father)*
*Reatha M. Anderson Powell (Biological Mother)*
*Johnny L. Powell, Jr (Brother)*
*Dovella Anderson West (Sister)*
*Lenora Anderson (Aunt)*
*George F. Owens, Sr (Father-in-Law Deceased)*
*Devaughn Williams (Father of Grandsons)*
*Indiana Department of Corrections*
*City of Lawrence, Indiana*
*New Wineskin Ministries, Indianapolis, IN*

# PROLOGUE

*To all the fathers who read these memoirs, I will always remember Father's Day. There is now a tradition of taking young men fishing which started back in 1986 with my five year old son and my Father-in-Law, the late George F. Owens, Sr. It's been over twenty-seven years and I still contact nephews, brothers, close friends and cousins to participate. I also ask them to gather up their sons, grandsons and nephews to spend the day at some fishing lake with us. George, my father-in-law who helped start this tradition has now passed on to Glory since the great age of 96.*

*But the rest of us still happily carry it on. We eagerly devour the sandwiches which my wife loves to make out of ham, turkey and bologna for the outing. She also places chips and pretzels in baggies and loads up a cooler with soft drinks and juices. The fishing excursion only lasts about five to six hours, but the fellowship lasts a lifetime. I enjoy the excitement from my grandsons as they start questioning "Where are we going fishing this year Papaw?" I also enjoy seeing the sparkle in their eyes and the smile on their faces when they finally catch a fish regardless of the size.*

*These priceless memories will go on forever regardless if we continue the tradition or not. However, I have no plans to discontinue the anticipation of where we will be from year to year.*

# ABOUT THE AUTHOR

# Rondle L. Anderson

*Rondle left the Indiana Department of Correction (IDOC) on April 1, 2009 after 32 years of continuous service. His last Executive Team position was the Northern Region Director of Operations. This position provided operational supervision to IDOC Superintendents assigned to the northern half of the State. Region Directors report directly to the Deputy*

*Commissioner of Operation for the Department. Rondle started with the Department of Correction in 1977 as a Correctional Officer and was then promoted through the ranks of Counselor, Group Leader, Casework Manager, Supervisor of Classification, Unit Team Manager, Assistant Superintendent, Facility Director, Superintendent, and as mentioned Region Director. He was also certified to instruct/facilitate Mid-Level Managers of IDOC on topics such as Cultural Competency, Basic Supervisory Leadership, and Interpersonal Communication Skills.*

*From 1997 thru 2000, Ron was selected by the National Institute of Correction to facilitate training in the areas of Diversity Leadership and Advanced Leadership Strategies for Women and Minorities.*

*Rondle received his Bachelor of Science Degree from Indiana University in Criminal Justice/Public Affairs and has accumulated numerous training credits from the National Institute of Corrections. He is a professional member of the American Correctional Association (ACA) and Past President of the Indiana Correctional Association (ICA), as well as the Indiana Chapter of the National Association of Blacks in Criminal Justice (NABCJ).*

*Rondle received recognition as the ICA Distinguished Service Award recipient in 2005 and the*

*Distinguished Hoosier Award recipient from Indiana Governor Mitchell E. Daniels, Jr in 2009.*

# ENDORSEMENTS

*I have recently discovered that leading a family is the hardest job a man can ever have. It takes around the clock leadership, teaching, forgiving, mentoring, loving, and most important, time and presence. Just as every executive needs to understand their goal, strategy, and responsibility, every father needs to know those things as well. In this book, these principles are highlighted, and also detail the importance of a Biblical and Godly presence from both the "Holy Father" and present father or father-figure in a child's life. The book also provides guidance to fathers such as myself, who want to develop positive characteristics in their children that will lead to them having successful lives and thrive in a world that does not have an issue teaching them how to live the way it (The World) wants them to....*

**Cameron Anderson**
*Son of Author*
*Gwinnett County, GA*

Through the Indiana Correctional Association (the Association's name at the time in 1993) I met Rondle Anderson. It did not take long to realize Ron had a mission to emphasize to others the importance of fatherhood and raising a child. Values such as accountability, trustworthiness, faith, humanity, responsibility, knowledge, and reverence were characteristics Ron used in his employment and networking with others to mentor his staff and be a positive role model. Even more impressive to me was his "strategic planning" capabilities, which can be used with compassion, understanding, and love in raising a child. Rondle's "kind heart" is left in this book for others to enjoy.

*Eric Hoch,* **President**
*HOCCS Community Corrections*
*Indianapolis, Indiana*

*Seasons of Four Fathers is a must read for men and women interested in mentoring young people. Although the author's focus is on young men, the lessons taught here can be applied to young women as well. You will be challenged to seriously consider your part in encouraging and helping young people to fulfill their God ordained destiny.*

**Evangelist Pamela Thomas**
*President,*
*Christ for the World Ministries*
*Indianapolis, Indiana*

*I have known Rondle Anderson for over thirty-five years. He is a natural leader who represents what it means to be a great father. His experience in the correctional field has given him extensive knowledge and wisdom on the problems facing young black men today. I am very proud of Rondle for his achievement in completing this book. I am sure that it will be a blessing to all who read it.*

**Marsha Hedgeman**
*Reading/English Instructor- Indianapolis Public Schools*
*Decatur Township Schools;*
*Equipping Pillar Leader*
*- New Wineskin Ministries Indianapolis, Indiana*

*Reading **Seasons of Four Fathers** by Rondle Anderson immediately took me back to my own childhood. It made me reminisce of all the fun times we had as a family but most of all it made me appreciate and understand the importance of the men in my family. How each of them impacted my life, good or bad, by example and words of wisdom.*

***Seasons of Four Fathers** is an easy read that is filled with great wisdom and practical examples to help fathers (biological fathers, step fathers, or father figures) understand the impact they make naturally and spiritually in a child's life. The world is in great need of more good natural and spiritual father figures to help steer kids away from the juvenile justice system towards excellence in the arena of education. I would recommend this book to men who desire to become fathers as well as those who are already fathers.*

*Pastor Erika N. McLaurin*
*New Wineskin Ministries International*
*School of Ministry Director*
*Indianapolis, Indiana*

Made in the USA
Middletown, DE
11 December 2025

24725140R00051